The Vajra and Bell

Vessantara

The Vajra and Bell

WINDHORSE PUBLICATIONS

Also by Vessantara
Meeting the Buddhas
Tales of Freedom
The Mandala of the Five Buddhas

Published by Windhorse Publications, 11 Park Road, Birmingham, B13 8AB
www.windhorsepublications.com

© Vessantara 2001

Printed by Interprint Ltd, Marsa, Malta
Cover design: Karmabandhu and Maria Allen
Cover images: vajra and bell © Clear Vision Trust Picture Archive; background image © Photodisc
Black and white illustrations by Aloka

A catalogue record for this book is available from the British Library.
ISBN 1 899579 41 9

Since this work is intended for a general readership, Pali and Sanskrit words have been transliterated without the diacritical marks which would have been appropriate in a work of a more scholarly nature.

CONTENTS

Illustration credits xi

Introduction 1

1 The Development of the Vajrayana 4

2 Taking up the Vajra and Bell 7

3 The Vajra as Diamond 9

4 The Vajra as Philosopher's Stone 12

5 The Vajra as Thunderbolt 14

6 The Vajra as Sceptre 16

7 The Vajra in Detail 18

8 The Bell – Sounding Wisdom 23

9 Bells and Their Uses 25

10 The Vajra-Bell as Emptiness 28

11 The Vajra-Bell as Mandala 30

12 Vajra and Bell Together 35

13 Vajra and Bell in Highest Tantra 37

14 The Vajrahumkara Mudra 42

15 Ritual Uses of the Vajra and Bell 43

16 The Double Vajra 45

17 Ritual Implements and Mandalas 49

18 Holders of the Vajra 51

19 The Buddha Vajradhara 53

Conclusion 56

Notes and References 57

Index 59

Illustration credits

Plate 1. Vajra and bell, photograph by Terry Delamare, © Clear Vision Trust Picture Archive

Plate 2. Dhardo Rimpoche, photograph by Kulamitra, © Clear Vision Trust Picture Archive

Plate 3. Glass vajra, photograph by Vic Burnside, courtesy of Vajragupta and the Birmingham Buddhist Centre

Plate 4. © Photodisc

Plate 5. © De Beers Group

Plate 6. The British sovereign's sceptre with cross, 1661. Crown copyright: Historic Royal Palaces

Plate 7. Photograph by Suvajra, © Clear Vision Trust Picture Archive

Plate 8. Bells at a Greek Orthodox Church, Getty Images, © Photodisc

About the Author

Vessantara is a senior member of the Western Buddhist Order. Born Tony McMahon in London in 1950, he gained an MA in English at Cambridge University. Interested in Buddhism since his teens, he first had direct contact with Buddhists in 1971. In 1974 he became a member of the Western Buddhist Order and was given the name Vessantara, which means 'universe within'. In 1975 he gave up a career in social work to become chairman of the Brighton Buddhist Centre. Since then he has divided his time between meditating, studying, and aiding the development of several Buddhist centres, including retreat centres in England, Wales, and Spain.

For six years he was secretary to Sangharakshita, the founder of the Western Buddhist Order, and for seven years he led three-month courses for people entering the Order.

He is much in demand as a Buddhist teacher, giving talks and leading retreats and workshops in Europe and Australasia. He is now based in Birmingham, where he works as one of a group of Order members to whom Sangharakshita has passed on his responsibilities.

ACKNOWLEDGEMENTS

In my descriptions of the vajra and bell and their uses I have drawn on many sources. I am particularly grateful to Sangharakshita and to Dagyab Kyabgon Rimpoche for the explanations they have given me over the years. I am also indebted to Robert Beer for the excellent way in which he has drawn together material on the vajra and bell in his book, *The Encyclopedia of Tibetan Symbols and Motifs*.[1] Some of my other sources are referenced at the end of the book.

My text has benefited very much from the attentions of my friends at Windhorse Publications, and all the readers who have commented on the text at its different stages. I want particularly to thank Jnanasiddhi, a writer's dream of a commissioning editor, for her clarity and encouragement.

Lastly, I wrote much of the first draft in New Zealand, in a small kuti at the bottom of the garden of my friends Purna and Malini. I am grateful to them for all their kindness, and for providing me with the garden scents and idyllic sea views that helped to enrich my writing.

INTRODUCTION

ALTHOUGH I HAD CONSIDERED myself a Buddhist for some time, my first meeting with other Buddhists was in 1971, when I travelled to Scotland to visit Samye Ling, which was one of the first Tibetan Buddhist centres to be founded in Europe. While I was there, Kalu Rimpoche arrived. He was an extraordinary old man who had spent many years meditating in solitude, and had become a great meditation teacher. Most of the lamas who had come to the West at that time were young, and were adapting (rather too well in one or two cases) to Western culture. Kalu Rimpoche was a traditionalist, which occasionally led to interesting culture clashes. For instance, when travelling by plane he had been known to bemuse cabin crews by throwing rice around to bless the aircraft.

I well remember sitting in the shrine-room at Samye Ling for the first puja in which Kalu Rimpoche and the monks who accompanied him took part. I understood not a single word, and there was no explanation of what we were doing. Like a beginner who can pick out a couple of tunes on the piano, I could just recognize one or two of the mantras that we chanted. Nevertheless I was deeply moved. Doubtless I was affected by the esotericism of it all: the maroon robes of the monks, the colourful room with its magical paintings and statues, the incomprehensible chanting that allowed my imagination free rein as to its significance, and the Wise Old Man from Tibet around whom everything revolved. Such feelings are natural but tend to wear off with familiarity.

However, underneath those superficial responses to what for me at the time was unusual and exotic, there was a much deeper and more long-lasting response. As I sat trying to concentrate and open myself to what was happening, I was affected by a number of aspects of what I experienced. There was the resonant chanting, not musical by Western standards, but elemental and shifting in mood, like a stream flowing over mountain rocks, through dense forests and sunlit meadows, never stopping. There were the *mudras* – the symbolic gestures – a dance of the hands, taking endless forms, graceful, and again flowing.

From both the chanting and the mudras I received a sense of change and changelessness together. The voices rose and fell, raced and slowed, were constantly changing, yet all these effects were always and only the breath. Similarly, the hands displayed the shapes of all kinds of offerings: food and drink, flowers, lights, and so on; they expressed devotion towards higher forces and threat to hindering ones. They produced whole worlds to offer to the Buddhas and other Enlightened beings. They brought them into existence for a fraction of a second, or at most a minute or two, then dissolved them away once more, always to be replaced by something else. Yet these worlds were being created always and only by the power of the mind expressed through the fingers.

And nestling in the hands of each monk during much of this performance (one that was entirely natural, with no element of the theatrical) were two ritual objects. In their right hands they held a small bronze sceptre – the vajra. In their left hands they each held a bell, the handle of which was half a vajra. At times the ringing of the vajra-bell was supplemented by the rattle of the *damaru* – a small double-sided drum whose sound suggested the chattering teeth of some huge skeleton.

Of all my memories of that shrine-room, it is the sound of the vajra-bells that I recall most clearly. The bells all had slightly different tones, and Kalu Rimpoche's had a piercing beauty that seemed to wipe my mind free of all thoughts. It was so intense that it hurt my ears, and my body wanted it to stop, yet it also felt like the most real experience of my life, and my mind wanted it to go on for ever. Although so many years have passed, I feel as if the sound of that bell has never quite stopped resounding inside me.

The vajra and bell that Kalu Rimpoche used in his meditations are central symbols of Tibetan Buddhism. The aim of this third book in Windhorse Publications' series on Buddhist symbols is to introduce them and to give an idea of the part they play in Tibetan Buddhism, as well as of ways in which readers can come to appreciate their meaning and significance. (The vajra also appears in Chinese and Japanese Buddhism, for example in the Japanese Shingon School, but a consideration of Far Eastern Buddhism is beyond the scope of this book.) As we shall see, the symbolism of the vajra and bell is extremely rich. In fact I shall not be able to do it full justice in the course of a short book. Not only that, the vajra and bell are such central symbols for Tibetan Buddhism that I shall need to introduce some of the background of the Buddhist Tantra.

In writing about Buddhist Tantra it is always difficult to know how much to say. Some matters are traditionally reserved for those who have received the appropriate initiation. At the same time, a writer cannot ignore the fact that most of what was traditionally kept hidden is now available on the shelves of many large bookstores in the West. So I have tried to steer a middle course, not going into too much detail in some areas, but allowing myself to discuss matters on which information is already freely available.

I have written about the vajra and bell before, in my much larger book called *Meeting the Buddhas*.[2] That book was an introduction to the main symbolic figures that are meditated upon in the Indo-Tibetan tradition, some of whom are visualized holding a vajra and/or a bell. I shall cover that ground again only very briefly, and concentrate mainly on the vajra and bell as ritual objects. I shall give my account of them with a broad spread of readers in mind. For those of you who use vajras and bells in your practice of Tibetan Buddhism I hope it will deepen your appreciation of what you hold in your hands. And for those of you practising, or considering practising, in other Buddhist traditions, I hope that learning about these very important symbols will provide you with inspiration. May contemplating the vajra and bell inspire us all to develop deep compassion and wisdom, and all the other qualities that are represented by these two objects.

1

THE DEVELOPMENT OF THE VAJRAYANA

THE VAJRA, as we shall see in more detail later, is a symbolic sceptre that has the properties of both a diamond and a thunderbolt. It is an ancient symbol, associated with prehistoric cults of a supreme sky god, or sometimes with a thunder deity.[3] In Western Europe the thunderbolt was often envisaged as a brilliant axe hurled by the sky god, cleaving a path through the air. In Greek mythology, the thunderbolt was the great weapon of Zeus, ruler of the heavens, who became supreme among gods and men after he overthrew his father Cronus and defeated the Titans. In Norse mythology, thunder was the sound made by the mighty hammer wielded by the god Thor.

In ancient India the thunderbolt-wielding deity was Indra, a god of sky and monsoon rain, who appears in the Vedas. He was often depicted as robust and powerful, riding an elephant, and brandishing a thunderbolt in the form of a vajra. This vajra was depicted as a sceptre with a central axis and an arched cluster of prongs at each end.[4] As we shall see, Buddhism took over this powerful symbol, and turned it towards the purpose of gaining Enlightenment. This is symbolized in a Buddhist legend in which the Buddha Shakyamuni took the vajra-thunderbolt from Indra, and forced its wrathful open prongs together to fashion a peaceful sceptre.

In early Buddhism the vajra was wielded by Vajirapani. He appears in the early Buddhist texts as a kind of personal daemon of the Buddha. In the *Ambattha Sutta* of the Pali Canon, the Buddha challenges a young and haughty Brahmin called Ambattha who has been insulting him and describing as 'menials' the Shakya clan into which he was born. The Buddha puts the young man on the spot by asking whether it is correct that Ambattha is himself descended from a Shakyan slave girl. Ambattha refuses to reply, for he knows that what the Buddha says is true. The Buddha asks him three times, and at the third time of asking, Vajirapani, 'holding a huge iron club, flaming, ablaze and glowing, up in the sky just above Ambattha, was thinking: "If this young man Ambattha does not answer … I'll split his head into seven pieces."' Wisely, Ambattha answers the question, acknowledging that the Buddha is correct.[5]

Vajirapani and the vajra make only rare appearances in the Pali Canon. The vajra is referred to more frequently in the Mahayana sutras. For example, one of the most important of the Perfection of Wisdom sutras is the *Vajracchedika*. Usually referred to in English as the *Diamond Sutra*, its name suggests it is the sutra 'that cuts like a diamond' – cutting off all wrong concepts about reality and the suffering that they cause.

The vajra really came into its own with the development of Buddhist Tantra. Some time around the second century of the common era, texts known as tantras started to appear which advocated new methods of spiritual practice. These new practices included the use of symbolic ritual, a strong emphasis on the guru and on initiation, the visualization of deities, imaginative identification with the Enlightened state, the use of mandala patterns, and the recitation of mantras.

In the early Tantric texts, classified into *Kriya* and *Carya* Tantras, there is no suggestion that these methods should be used to gain Enlightenment. Instead, they are magical ways to attain mundane goals such as curing illness or controlling the weather. At this stage the Buddhist Tantra is usually called the Mantrayana – the path of mantra (the recitation of symbolic sound).[6]

The vajra appears in some of these early Tantric texts. For example, one Kriya Tantra text describes a mandala (a sacred space, usually the abode of Buddhas or other figures, that is visualized in meditation) containing three 'families', or symbolic groupings. The central group is the Buddha family, and these figures are flanked by a Lotus family and a Vajra family. However, only the figures in the Buddha family are seen as Enlightened. The vajra still has a peripheral place in the scheme of things.

As the centuries passed and Buddhist Tantra developed, the vajra increased in importance, until finally, perhaps by the late seventh century, the vajra had become the central symbol of Buddhist Tantra, which then became known as the Vajrayana – the way of the diamond thunderbolt. The system of arranging Buddhas in symbolic patterns also developed further, until eventually an arrangement of Five Buddhas appeared, known as the Vajradhatu Mandala – the 'Sacred Circle of the Sphere of the Diamond Thunderbolt'.[7]

In the final stages of the development of the Tantra, not only was the Vajra family seen as consisting of Enlightened figures, it had become the central family of the mandala. Thus most of the central figures of the Highest or Anuttarayoga Tantra – the most developed form of Buddhist Tantra – are associated with the Vajra family. In these tantras the Buddha Akshobhya, the head of Vajra family, moves to the centre of the mandala of the five Buddha families.

Figures associated with the vajra also increased in importance, and were given higher status, as time went on. For instance Vajrapani (whose name means 'Thunderbolt in Hand') first appeared in Buddhist texts as a *yaksha* – a kind of powerful nature-spirit. Over the centuries he came to be regarded as a Bodhisattva, associated with the liberated energy of the Enlightened Mind. Finally, as we shall see later, he became a Buddha, and a central figure in later Buddhist Tantra, in the form of Vajradhara – 'Holder of the Thunderbolt'.[8]

I am not aware of any research into the origins of the bell as a Buddhist symbol. It probably first appeared independently of the vajra, then – as the vajra gained impor-tance – the bell acquired a vajra-handle, and finally the vajra and vajra-bell were paired as ritual implements and became the attributes of various Enlightened beings.

2

TAKING UP THE VAJRA AND BELL

NOW THAT WE HAVE GAINED a little background to the development of the vajra and bell, and the Vajrayana in which they feature so prominently, it is time to gain a feeling for the vajra and bell themselves.

The vajra is a metal sceptre, golden in colour, perhaps three inches long. (See illustration on page 19.) It has an oval hub in the middle, with a central prong or axis running through it. At each of its two symmetrical ends there are a number of prongs that arch out from the central one and then curve back to meet it again. These prongs can be two, four, or eight in number. In this book we shall concentrate on the so-called five-pronged vajra, as this is the most common form used as a hand-implement in Tantric ritual. The bell is about three or so inches in diameter at its rim, also usually made of bronze. Its handle consists of a half vajra, below which is a female face wearing a five-pointed crown.

I shall describe both the vajra and bell in more detail later, but this description should be enough to give you a general impression of them. To take that further, perhaps you could now visualize sitting with a vajra and bell in front of you (or, if you actually possess an vajra and bell, you could put them out and contemplate them.) Whether in imagination or reality, pick up the vajra and bell, and feel their cool weight in your hands. The vajra always goes in your right hand; the bell in your left.

In starting to gain a feeling for these powerful symbols, we shall begin by focusing on the vajra in our right hand, and feeling its qualities. It has the attributes of a diamond, the philosopher's stone, a thunderbolt, and a royal sceptre. We can meditate on each of these in turn.

3

THE VAJRA AS DIAMOND

LET THE VAJRA rest in your right hand, turning your middle and ring fingers inwards to press its oval hub gently into your palm. Feel the contours of the arching prongs.

Now open out your hand so that your palm is facing upwards with the vajra lying horizontally upon it. Contemplate the vajra for a little while, then imagine that it turns into a diamond, a brilliant gem, burning like a star in your right palm. All kinds of colours appear as you move your hand at different angles. Yet the gem that is creating ephemeral beauty as it reflects light to your eyes is itself unchanging.

The word *vajra* is Sanskrit, and one of its principal meanings is 'diamond'. One of the main symbolic qualities of the vajra is that it resembles a diamond – in its beauty, but especially in its immutability. Diamond is the hardest natural substance known to man. It is over three times as hard as its nearest rival, corundum. Thus it is used to cut other stones. Formed under intense pressure over vast periods of time at depths sometimes in excess of seventy-five miles, it will endure unchanged over ages. Diamonds are forever, as the saying goes, which is why they are used in wedding rings to symbolize a lasting union. But even the most steadfast union is unlikely to outlast by long its diamond anniversary, and Buddhism is concerned with going beyond all forms of mundane existence.

Buddhism can be seen as a quest for what is permanently satisfying, for what really endures. This quest for what is permanent inevitably involves becoming intensely aware of impermanence. The momentary glint of colour as you turn a diamond in your hand, the few decades of a human relationship, the vast span of time for which a diamond abides, all come to an end. It is in the nature of things that whatever is compounded – made up of parts – will sooner or later be broken up and become unrecognizable. Unfortunately, it is the habit of the human mind to ignore this. Although intellectually we are aware of the law of impermanence, emotionally we are usually in denial. We crave love, power, status, possessions, and so forth. If we watch our mind closely we shall see that we treat these things as if they will give us permanent happiness. Not only that, we imbue the world with a permanence that it does not possess. We tend to see things as solid and real. We often treat people and possessions as if they were fixed, as if they existed in and of themselves, when they are actually impermanent, appearing and then passing away in dependence upon a whole mass of conditions, as ungraspable as the brief fire of colour that burns within our turning diamond.

Through exploring the impermanent nature of what is compounded, Buddhism aims to lead us to what is permanently satisfying. As the Buddha once proclaimed to his monks:

> There exists, monks, that which is unborn, that which is unbecome, that which is uncreated, that which is unconditioned. For if there were not, monks, this which is unborn, that which is unbecome, that which is uncreated, that which is unconditioned, there would not be made known here the escape from that which is born, from that which is become, from that which is created, from that which is conditioned.[9]

This unborn and not-compounded is not something to be found in some distant galaxy. It is right here and now. To find it we simply have to use our minds in a radically different way from their usual diffuse and restless mode of functioning. We need to develop deep concentration, and then use that focused consciousness to explore the nature of life and the mind. Through a radical penetration of the truth of impermanence we shall come to recognize that time and space are functions of consciousness. We shall see into reality itself, and that eternal truth will set us free.

See the diamond in your right hand change back into a vajra, but retain the sense that it has all the qualities of a diamond. In particular, try to gain a feeling for the vajra's diamond-like immutability. It symbolizes a state of consciousness that is unborn, unchanging, forever satisfying. The vajra's inability to be cut or divided, like the powerful bonding of the diamond's carbon atoms that enables it to cut all other stones, is a potent symbol for the uncompounded, indivisible nature of the Enlightened Mind.

4

THE VAJRA AS PHILOSOPHER'S STONE

NOW IMAGINE that the vajra in your hand transforms into the philosopher's stone. This was a stone or substance that followers of the Western alchemical tradition believed would be capable of turning base metals into gold. Of course the search for the philosopher's stone failed, though it was only in the nineteenth century that it was conclusively proved that it is impossible to transmute the elements in this way. But this fruitless quest provided much of the equipment and basic research for what was to become modern chemistry. None the less, the philosopher's stone remains a powerful symbol on a psychological and spiritual level. *Vajra* was translated into Tibetan as *dorje* – 'lord of stones'. So for Tibetan Buddhism the vajra is the lord of stones that transmutes the base metal of our everyday self into the gold of an Enlightened being. Held in your hand it symbolizes the power to transform all your experience into richness and beauty.

I have been fortunate enough to see many beautiful things in my life. I have experienced the splendour of Mount Kanchenjunga and the vista of the Himalayas. I have entered the cool and tranquil perfection of the Alhambra. I have viewed many of Monet's finest paintings, and visited his natural masterpiece, the riot of life and colour of his garden at Giverny. However, probably the most beautiful things I have ever seen were a couple of margarine tubs in the kitchen of an old Welsh cottage after a particularly good meditation on a solitary retreat in the 1980s. It is the mind that transmutes the base metal of experience into gold, and gold into base metal. If we are depressed, a walk in the park on a glorious day may just leave us feeling alienated from people who are able to enjoy the experience. If we are in love, we may well be singing in the rain. If we refine our mental states through meditation and other practices we increasingly experience beauty in the everyday. More than that, as we come to understand the nature of reality we see that impermanence allows for the possibility of total transformation. Because there is nothing about us that is fixed and permanent, we can work over time to improve any aspect of ourselves. Spiritually speaking, there is no base metal that cannot be transmuted into gold.

Buddhism sees human beings as having three main aspects: body, speech, and mind. Buddhist Tantra aims to bring about a total transformation of all these aspects of ourselves by engaging all three in its rituals and meditations. The body is involved through making mudras and using ritual implements such as the vajra and bell, the speech through chanting ritual texts and mantras, and the mind through visualizing realms of light in which you encounter, or become, one or more Enlightened beings. Thus there is a very satisfying completeness about this form of Buddhist practice.

For Tantric Buddhism the ideal person is the *mahasiddha* – the great Tantric adept. These are men and women who have brought about an alchemical transformation of their energy, refining it repeatedly through Tantric meditation and ritual. As a result they have developed *siddhi* – magical attainments. These are of two kinds. Mundane siddhi are supernormal powers such as telepathy, flying, and other kinds of miraculous feats. The highest siddhi are the transformation of the mind and emotions into the transcendental wisdom and compassion of an Enlightened being.

Imagine the philosopher's stone changing back into the vajra, but retain the sense that the vajra is a magical implement, capable of transforming anything: the darkest dross of your mind, the most ingrained habits, the worst of you, into energy that can promote your spiritual awakening. Because everything is impermanent, there is nothing fixed and final about ourselves at all. Every aspect of what we think of as 'me' can be refined and wrought into finer and finer forms. The vajra symbolizes this capacity that we all possess to transform ourselves totally.

5

THE VAJRA AS THUNDERBOLT

NEXT, WE ARE GOING TO SEE the vajra turning into a thunderbolt. Before doing so you might prefer to imagine yourself transformed into some kind of storm god or goddess, for the handling of lightning is not for mere mortals. A typical lightning flash involves a potential difference between cloud and ground of several million volts. Not only that, it can reach temperatures of around 50,000°F, or about six times the heat of the visible surface of the Sun. Try to imagine holding that power in your hand.

The word *vajra* means thunderbolt as well as diamond. It is extraordinary that the same Sanskrit word came to be applied to two such completely different experiences. The diamond is one of the most immutable and long-lasting substances we know of, while a bolt of lightning lasts only a fraction of a second.

In that fifth of a second or so for which you see a flash of lightning, everything is lit up. In the case of nocturnal storms, the curtain of darkness is rent apart and the whole landscape is temporarily illuminated and revealed. Thus the vajra as thunderbolt becomes a symbol for what tears asunder the veil of ignorance and enables you to see things as they really are.

For Buddhism what brings this about is *prajna*, insight into reality. Having developed a calm and concentrated mind, you begin to reflect on the characteristics of reality as described by the Buddha and other teachers who have seen into its true nature. For example, you might contemplate the 'three marks of conditioned existence': its imper-manence, its lack of any permanently satisfying experience, and its insubstantiality – how it is devoid of any fixed inherent selfhood. When you first contemplate these things your experience of them is mediated by words or images. But if you continue to deepen your focus upon them, perhaps over a number of years, there eventually comes a moment in which you intuitively apprehend their truth. You leave behind words and images and enter a direct, naked experience of their reality.

This experience is *prajna*, and to start with it comes in momentary flashes, in which the truth dawns like lightning. As time goes on, these flashes become more frequent and start as it were to join up. Eventually your whole life is illumined by the light of this profound wisdom. The vajra as thunderbolt symbolizes this insight that destroys all ignorance.

Taking this a stage further, the thunderbolt appears in many cultures as a weapon. Obviously no human being could harness and direct such power, so as we saw earlier the thunderbolt is the attribute of many powerful divinities, such as Zeus and Thor. For Buddhist Tantra the vajra is the perfect weapon that overcomes ignorance and the suffering it causes. It is described as having three main attributes: it cannot be used frivolously, it never fails to hit (and destroy) its target, and it always returns to its owner's hand.[10] Prajna, transcendental insight, has all these qualities. It is an experi-ence of what is truly real, transcending time and space, an experience that is not dependent on mundane causes and conditions. Thus it cannot be used in any frivolous way; indeed it cannot be put at the service of the ego at all. When prajna comes into contact with delusion and wrong views it has a shattering effect upon them, leaving you far freer than before. Nothing mundane can withstand it. In that sense it never fails to hit its target. Once attained, transcendental insight can never be lost. It becomes a natural part of how you experience the world. In that sense it always returns to your hand.

Allow the thunderbolt to change back into the vajra once more, but retain the sense that it has all the qualities of the thunderbolt of prajna: illuminating everything, having tremendous energy, and capable of destroying all untruth and delusion, unerringly demolishing all the causes of suffering.

6

THE VAJRA AS SCEPTRE

FINALLY, IMAGINE THAT THE VAJRA in your hand turns into a royal sceptre. Feel yourself endowed with all the qualities of a monarch. To take the UK as an example, kings and queens at their coronation are invested with an orb and sceptre as symbols of their authority. The orb represents the cosmos or universe as a harmonious whole, and became a symbol of the power invested in the ruler; similarly the sceptre is a ceremonial rod or staff, and over the centuries it became symbolic of the power of command.

The vajra as royal sceptre is a symbol of authority in the spiritual world. Much of the symbolism of Tantric empowerment is related to coronation or royal investiture. For example, in ancient India kings were 'crowned' by a kind of baptism. Water from a number of pots was poured over them, to symbolize the fact that they were receiving all the powers of the realm. This became incorporated into Tantric initiation ritual. The first of the four Great Initiations of the Highest Tantra is the vase initiation, during which an empowered vase is placed on the crown of your head. Later, in the Vajra Master initiation, a vajra and bell are placed in your hands. Thus Tantric empowerment is sometimes described in the Tibetan Buddhist tradition as becoming like a king or queen.

As the royal sceptre turns back into the vajra, feel that it bestows upon you all the powers of spiritual sovereignty. In fact, you are becoming much more than an ordinary monarch, for the symbolism of coronation usually involves being empowered to rule by a deity. However, a central concept of Buddhist Tantra is what is known as 'taking the Goal as the path'. In some forms of Tantric practice you become, in your imagination, an Enlightened Being. That imaginative identification with the state of complete freedom, wisdom, and compassion, has far-reaching effects on your consciousness. It is fundamental to all forms of Buddhism that what you set your mind upon you tend to become. So over time, through imagining yourself as Enlightened, you increasingly become so in reality. Thus in some forms of Tantric initiation you are, as it were, enthroned as a Buddha or Bodhisattva by the Buddhas and Bodhisattvas. The vajra and bell in your hands represent this path of practice; they also symbolize your potential to become Enlightened, to reach a state in which the Dharma reigns supreme in your heart, holding sway throughout the realm of your consciousness.

In Buddhist Tantra, the vajra, and the right hand side of the body, are associated with the masculine. Therefore it is interesting to reflect that these four aspects of the vajra – diamond, philosopher's stone, thunderbolt, and royal sceptre – correspond very well to the four main masculine archetypes identified by the Jungian psychologists Robert Moore and Douglas Gillette.[11] In their work with their clients, and their exploration of myth and symbol, they found four deep patternings which they considered to be inherent in the male psyche. These four archetypes related to the King, whose positive functions are to bring order and to bless; the Warrior, who strives courageously for the good; the Magician, who represents the archetype of transformation; and the Lover, whose attributes bring one into positive and appreciative relatedness with the world and with other people.

We have seen that the vajra is a royal sceptre – an attribute of the king; it is a thunderbolt – a weapon for the warrior; it is also a philosopher's stone – an alchemical tool of transformation for the magician; finally, it is a diamond – the symbol of the faithful lover.

7

THE VAJRA IN DETAIL

STILL HOLDING THE VAJRA in your hand, imagine now examining its different aspects. In the middle is a rounded hub. (In some vajras it may be spherical, or the sphere may be flattened into more of an oval or egg-shape.) On each side of this central hub, above and below, the elements of the design are exactly repeated, so we shall look at one end of the vajra, knowing that it is replicated at the other. Above the central hub is a set of three rings in the shape of strings of pearls. Out of these grow eight lotus petals, surmounted by moon mats. Outside these is a further set of pearl rings. Beyond these, the vajra opens out with the central axis and four curved prongs. These curved prongs grow out of the mouths of strange creatures called *makaras*, and then curl inwards to rejoin the central axis near its tip.

The elements of the vajra are themselves very rich in symbolism, and I am not going to attempt an exhaustive presentation. The Buddha's teachings were preserved orally for many centuries. To aid the work of memorizing, many teachings were reduced to handy numerical lists. This was very useful, both as a mnemonic, and to allow for the growth of a whole numerical symbolism. The difficulty for a writer is that objects with, say, eight petals or ten prongs will have symbolic resonances with many lists of eight and ten preserved in the Buddhist teachings, so rather than give long lists of correspondences, some of which will not mean much to the average reader, I shall take a cross-section, as it were, through the complex symbolism of the vajra, and pick out some of the main elements.

The central sphere or hub of the vajra represents the *dharmata* – the sphere of reality itself. It is impossible to say anything about this experience without falsifying it, because it is beyond space and time, and all our concepts, and even our metaphors, draw on experience within those dimensions. When you experience the *dharmata*, you encounter the ultimate truth about the world, and (to the extent that you can talk about them as separate) the ultimate nature of consciousness.

The three pearl rosaries stand for three means of entering into that sphere of reality, known as the three doors of liberation. You enter these states of transcendental freedom by contemplating one or another of the Three Marks, the common qualities that Buddhism sees in all mundane experience.

Firstly, through penetrating deeply into the truth of universal impermanence you enter the *animitta samadhi* – the transcendental concentration on signlessness. This is a state in which all words and concepts about things drop away. Words and concepts are attempts to fix things, and they are all as it were carried off by the flood of universal impermanence. This experience is one in which everything is experienced in terms of energy, ungraspable, as there are no fixed things to take hold of.

Secondly, through contemplation of the unsatisfactoriness of conditioned existence you enter the *apranihita samadhi* – the transcendental concentration on directionless-ness. This is a state of perfect equanimity. Through seeing that no mundane experience can provide you with any lasting happiness and that being involved with it always entails suffering sooner or later, you emotionally disengage yourself from it. In that state you are no longer pulled and pushed by the forces of attraction and aversion that drove you when you still believed that mundane existence could satisfy you. So you are in a state of perfect spiritual stability and balance.

Thirdly, through contemplating the absence of intrinsic selfhood of all phenomena, you enter the *shunyata samadhi* – transcendental concentration on emptiness. This follows on from the vision of universal impermanence. As you can find no fixed, unchanging essence to anything, everything is devoid of any kind of intrinsic selfhood – including you. Although this revelation that you and all things have no true existence may sound frightening to those who have not experienced it, in reality it is very liberating. As we have seen, this absence of inherent existence means there is nothing about you that cannot be transformed. Also this fixed self that we imagine ourselves to be is the cause of all our suffering. We are constantly checking that we are safe and secure, and our energy constantly revolves around thoughts, hopes, and fears concerning this 'me'. When this fixed 'me' is seen to be a deeply-held illusion, that tight mass of energy is released in a great outpouring of gratitude that the source of suffering has been seen through, and of love for all life, from which one had been separated by this illusory but seemingly-solid barrier of separate selfhood.

Next we come to a section of the vajra whose symbolism concerns the Bodhisattva – the person who is committed to gaining Enlightenment not for themselves alone but out of the compassionate desire to help all living beings. Above and below these pearl rings grow eight lotuses. The upper petals stand for an archetypal set of eight great Bodhisattvas, and the lower ones for their female consorts.[12] A full-moon disc above each of the lotuses suggests the seats on which the Bodhisattvas and their consorts are placed. It also represents the full realization of the Bodhicitta, the mind or heart of Enlightenment – what essentially makes a Bodhisattva a Bodhisattva – in its aspects of both wisdom and compassion. Working our way outwards from the central hub, we now find more sets of rings, three above and three below. These symbolize the six perfections: generosity, ethics, patience, effort, meditation, and wisdom, that are the primary spiritual practices of a Bodhisattva.

Now the ends of the vajra open out. Around the central prong at each end grow four others, all emerging from the mouths of makaras. Makaras are sea-creatures found in ancient Indian iconography. They are a composite of a number of animals, but their most significant and clearly-defined feature when they appear on the vajra is that they have the jaws of crocodiles. Like bulldogs, crocodiles are known for the power of their jaws, and for their refusal to release their grip on their prey until it is dead. Thus these four makaras can be seen as symbols of effort and persistence in Dharma practice. We need to hold on (like grim death if necessary) to the question of the nature of reality until it is seen clearly, and suffering is dead.

The composite nature of the makara also suggests that we as human beings are a strange mixture of different drives and tendencies. If our psychological make-up could be represented in animal terms we too might appear to have the eyes of a monkey, the tusks and ears of a wild boar, the jaws of a crocodile, and so on. Part of the task of Dharma practice is to use awareness and effort to bring our divergent tendencies together, so that eventually they are all engaged in the effort to destroy suffering, both our own and that of others.

The five prongs at each end, viewed end on, form a kind of mandala pattern. The upper set represents the Five Buddhas of the Vajradhatu Mandala. There is the white Buddha Vairocana, the blue Akshobhya, the yellow Ratnasambhava, the red Amitabha, and the green Amoghasiddhi. The lower set symbolizes their five female consorts of corresponding colours: Akashadhateshvari, Locana, Mamaki, Pandaravasini, and Tara.

There is a very rich symbolism associated with these figures. Their primary significance is as embodiments of the Five Wisdoms, which represent ways in which the Enlightened mind experiences things. The mirror-like wisdom symbolized by Akshobhya's consort, Locana, reflects everything objectively without the clouding and distorting effect of a belief in a fixed self confronting inherently-existing objects. The wisdom of sameness, symbolized by Ratnasambhava's consort Mamaki, recognizes the unity of all things as dependent arisings and reflections of consciousness. The discriminating wisdom, symbolized by Amitabha's consort Pandaravasini, sees the uniqueness of everything, that every moment of experience is, as it were, an unrepeatable offer. The all-accomplishing wisdom, symbolized by Amoghasiddhi's consort Tara, represents the active tendency in the heart of wisdom to act for the benefit of all beings, and the effectiveness of compassionate action that springs from transcendental wisdom. All four spring from the wisdom of the *dharmadhatu* – the sphere of reality – symbolized by Vairocana's consort Akashadhateshvari, that cognizes ultimate reality itself, just as the four outer prongs can be said to spring from the central axis.[13]

In this section I have been able to give only an outline of the complex symbolism contained in the details of the vajra. They embody the whole path and goal of Buddhist Tantra, and one could meditate on them indefinitely. As we shall see when we come to consider the vajra and bell together, there are yet more symbolic meanings to be found in the vajra than those we have examined so far. Before doing so, it is time to turn our attention from our right hand to our left, to explore the vajra-bell.

8

THE BELL — SOUNDING WISDOM

AS MENTIONED EARLIER, in Vajrayana ritual the vajra-bell is always held in the left hand. In imagination or reality, lift the bell and hear the sound the clapper makes as it rolls across the rim. Now place the forefinger of your left hand on top of the bell, where the central prong extends out from the vajra-handle. Hold the bell vertical, and listen to the silence. Then ring the bell by rotating your wrist. Hear the thrilling beauty of the sound, and allow your mind to follow it. Then return the bell to the upright position, and listen as the sound continues, taking many seconds to gradually die away. Sense the reverberations, growing ever more subtle, the sound rippling outwards like waves from a stone dropped into a lake. Follow the sound into the depths of silence.

When you have emerged from the silence, reflect a little on the effects of ringing the vajra-bell. Do those delicate undulations of sound ever stop? Or do they continue indefinitely, having effects however infinitesimal? Is the universe the same as it was before, or is it permanently altered? Taking your action in ringing the vajra-bell as an example, consider the effects of actions in general.

Now that we have taken up the vajra-bell and listened to its sound, it is time to reflect more upon it. We shall start by trying to gain some feeling for the vajra-bell just as bell, for although the vajra-bell is given many special meanings within the Vajrayana, it still retains the symbolism common to bells in general. So we shall start our reflections on the vajra-bell by coming down to earth – reflecting on how bells are made and their functions outside the Tantric context.

9

BELLS AND THEIR USES

BELLS ARE MADE from bell metal, a type of bronze, an alloy of copper and tin, with a small admixture of zinc and lead. They are cast by pouring molten metal into a mould consisting of an inner core and an outer mould, or cope, contoured to the bell's profile. Most moulds are faced with loam, but those for hand bells such as vajra-bells use sand instead. The liquid metal is heated to about 2,000°F before it enters the mould. Cooling is carefully controlled to prevent the outer surface from cooling faster than the inner, which would create tensions that could eventually cause cracking. Large bells require a week or two to cool. When the mould is removed, the rough cast of the bell is smoothed and polished. If a certain pitch is required, small amounts of metal can be ground from the bell's inner wall to give it the desired tone. For vajra-bells, the bell and handle are cast separately and joined together with pitch-resin.

Bells serve a number of functions. We shall explore these and see to what extent they apply to vajra-bells.

TO SUMMON OR ATTRACT ATTENTION
For example, bells are used in various religious traditions as a summons to worship, and the old English town-crier would ring his bell to attract attention so that he could make an announcement or deliver news. This is very much a function of the vajra-bell. In Tantra it is frequently used in order to summon, invite, or attract deities or other

figures to attend and participate in the functions of the ritual.

TO WARN OR DRIVE AWAY

In the West, church bells used to be rung to warn of dangers such as fire or invasion. These days alarm bells are still common, though being replaced by sirens and other kinds of horn. In earlier times bells were often placed on animals, buildings, or vehicles in order to ward off demons. In the Christian tradition, excommunications were performed with 'bell, book, and candle', and St Anthony Abbot is frequently portrayed with a bell attached to his crutch as a warning to demons. Similarly, the vajra-bell is sometimes rung vigorously in order to ward off or drive out forces or beings inimical to the purpose of the Tantric ritual.

TO REMIND AND AWAKEN

The English phrase 'that rings a bell' suggests calling to mind something previously experienced. In various spiritual traditions, for example in Gurdjieff groups or Vietnamese Zen, there is a practice of having a 'mindfulness bell' rung at intervals during activities. The purpose of the bell is to remind people of their purpose and of the need to remain aware. The vajra-bell is also used as a reminder of particular qualities or as an aid to awakening higher states of consciousness. For example, the vajra-bell may be rung during the recitation of the Vajrasattva mantra. Vajrasattva is an archetypal Buddha concerned essentially with purification, and the ringing of the vajra-bell is a reminder that everything is ultimately empty.[14] In general, the thrilling tone of the vajra-bell has a quality that tends to bring the mind into greater awareness.

AS MUSICAL INSTRUMENTS

Bells can be hung together in a tower, as a set known as a carillon, so that they can be played using a keyboard. Individual bells are sometimes used in musical settings. Vajra-bells also do duty as musical instruments in making offerings of music or sacred sound (*shabda* in Sanskrit) to please the Buddhas, Bodhisattvas, or other figures invoked during the ritual.

TO MARK THE PASSAGE OF TIME

Watches on ships are (or were) known as 'bells' because they were punctuated by half-hourly signals rung by the ship's bell. In monasteries and other places bells are used to regulate the day. However, vajra-bells are never used to mark the passage of time. On the contrary, their symbolism concerns what is timeless and immeasurable. In some societies, bells also have associations with a particular aspect of the passage of time: with the end of life, with funerals. It is the deceased person 'for whom the bell tolls'. But the vajra-bell is concerned with what transcends the mundane wheel of life and death.

It is to these aspects of the symbolism of the vajra-bell concerned with transcending time and space that we now turn, as we explore the specifically Tantric associations of the vajra-bell. As we shall see, it is a symbol of great complexity. Its two main meanings (when considered separately from the vajra) concern the sky as symbol of emptiness, and the mandala.

10

THE VAJRA-BELL AS EMPTINESS

IMAGINE (IF YOU CAN) holding the vault of the sky, vast and blue, in your left hand. The hollow of the bell is a container of empty space. It is related, by its shape, to the vault and consequently to the heavens. In fact, the symbolism of bells relates to earth and sky. The hanging position of the clapper means that it partakes of the symbolic significance of all objects which are suspended between heaven and earth. Indeed, the bell cannot sound unless it is lifted from the earth, allowing free movement of the clapper and preventing the damping effect of contact with the ground upon the rim.

As we have seen, when used by Tantric practitioners, the bell is always held in the left hand. In Buddhist Tantra, as we shall explore later, the left side of the body is associated with the feminine, and with wisdom. Thus the vajra-bell bears on its handle the face of the goddess Prajnaparamita, the Perfection of Wisdom, who is the female embodiment of the direct intuitive understanding of ultimate reality.[15]

Prajnaparamita as a goddess is the expression of the Prajnaparamita corpus of texts. These texts dealing with the Perfection of Wisdom are central to Mahayana Buddhism. They expound the emptiness of all phenomena. To the Western ear, this phrase may sound rather bleak, conjuring up images of greyness and meaninglessness. But as we have seen, nothing could be further from the truth. We need to understand what phenomena are empty of. They are empty, or devoid, of any fixed nature, any inherent existence. We routinely experience life in terms of fixed objects: a caterpillar, Marie, dental floss, the Kremlin, and so on. In this way we hold our conceptual world stable, and are able to exert a measure of control over it. However, in ultimate reality there are no fixed objects, nothing is finally under our control. Everything is an open-ended process, ungraspable. This applies equally to what we think of as 'me'. Thus we could say that the vajra-bell is a three-dimensional symbol for the ungraspable, unfixed nature of everything.

In Tantric Buddhism, space or the sky is used as the principal symbol for emptiness. Being itself infinite and ungraspable, it is an appropriate way to represent this 'open dimension' of all our experience. All phenomena arise and disappear, live and die, in dependence upon the appropriate conditions, and it is their inherent emptiness that enables this to happen. If a caterpillar had some fixed inherent nature as a caterpillar, it could never undergo its complete and radical transformation into a butterfly. Tantric visualization meditations dramatically represent the way in which everything is empty of inherent existence, produced by conditions. They do this by requiring the meditator to first visualize a vast, clear blue sky, and to reflect on it as a symbol of emptiness. Then, within the blue sky, various figures are visualized, not solid but made of light – figures of Buddhas, Bodhisattvas, and other Tantric deities. Finally, the whole phantasmagoria dissolves back into the blue sky, reinforcing the lesson that everything – even Buddhas – are empty of any inherent existence.

THE VAJRA-BELL AS MANDALA

IMAGINE HOLDING a whole world in your hand, the abode of enlightened beings, a mandala paradise created out of emptiness by enlightened consciousness. As we have seen, mandalas are sacred circles, ideal arrangements of elements around a central point of highest significance. In Tibetan Buddhism, the term mandala is employed in a number of situations, but principally to denote the harmonious world within which a Tantric deity is visualized. This mandala has many features: protective fences, cremation grounds, a mandala palace with all kinds of adornments, attendant goddesses and Bodhisattvas, and a central figure – the principal deity of the mandala. Amazingly enough, a whole mandala is symbolically represented by different details of the vajra-bell. Earlier we looked briefly at the main features of the bell, with its vajra-handle bearing the face of Prajnaparamita; now it is time to look at it in more detail, to see how these elements symbolize the different aspects of the mandala.

Vajra-bells differ in some of their smaller details, and there is not space in a short book like this to cover all the possible variations and their symbolism, so I shall describe my own vajra-bell, which has a form frequently found. We shall start from the bottom of the bell and work upwards. This corresponds to starting at the outer perimeter of the mandala and working inwards. Leaving the handle aside for the time being, the circumference of the bell gets narrower the higher up you look, thus the higher elements are closer to the centre of the mandala. (If this isn't clear to you, imagine looking down at a vajra-bell from above – which would be like looking at a two-dimensional mandala.)

The rim at the bottom of the bell corresponds to the disc of space. It is this rim that gives rise to the sound of emptiness. Similarly, when a mandala is visualized it is always seen as appearing out of vast blue sky, the space that symbolizes the emptiness of all phenomena. As we have seen, it is because everything is empty of any inherent existence, any fixed nature, that endless and total transformation is possible. It is emptiness that enables you to eventually transform your own mind into that of a Buddha.

If we move up a little from the rim we come to a ring of vajras, with a line above and below them. On a more expensive vajra-bell than mine, on which the details would be clearer, you would see that these two lines are actually strings of pearls circling the bell. These two rosaries of pearls and the circle of vajras represent the three circles of protection that guard and delimit the mandala. The lower of the two circles of pearls signifies the ring of wisdom flames that defends the outermost limit of the mandala. These flames are traditionally of five colours – white, yellow, red, green, and blue – associated with the wisdoms of the Five Buddhas of the mandala. These wisdom flames form a barrier that can only be passed if you are prepared to undergo the radical transformation brought about by transcendental wisdom.

Above the lower ring of pearls is the ring of vajras – all standing upright. On my vajra-bell there are forty-eight of them, plus a crossed vajra at the front. Sometimes there are fewer vajras in the ring – usually in multiples of eight or twelve. This ring of upright vajras stands for the great vajra fence and canopy that surrounds the mandala within the ring of wisdom flames. The vajras form an impenetrable barrier, preventing any inimical forces from entering.

The upper pearl rosary represents the third protection circle, made of lotuses. Like water lilies, lotuses grow out of the mud, rise upwards towards the light, and flower above the surface. Thus they have come to symbolize for Buddhism the development of higher states of consciousness. As the innermost circle of protection, the lotuses suggest that it is only when one is in a higher state of consciousness that one will be able to enter the mandala palace and encounter the embodiments of Enlightenment who dwell within it.

These three circles magically protect the mandala. Many associations with them can be made. For example, they can be related to an important set of Bodhisattvas known collectively as the Three Family Protectors. The flames are associated with Manjushri, the Bodhisattva who wields the flaming sword of wisdom; the vajras with Vajrapani, who embodies transcendental energy; and the lotuses with Avalokiteshvara, the Bodhisattva of Compassion. This emphasizes that it is spiritual qualities that are the only true protection. If your mind is filled with compassion, energy in pursuit of the good, and transcendental wisdom, then nothing can shake its tranquillity.

Next we come to a complex arrangement. Eight makaras (the strange composite creatures from whose mouths grew the outer prongs of the vajra) appear in the eight directions, holding in their mouths loops of jewelled pendants. These form a kind of frieze. Interspersed between the loop of jewels are eight vajras. These makaras are sometimes said to represent the eight great cremation grounds situated within the grounds of the mandala palace, or alternatively they represent the great crossed vajra on which the palace of the deity at the centre of the mandala rests. The loops of jewels stand for all the magnificent decorations on the outside of the mandala palace itself. The eight vajras are symbols of the eight great Bodhisattvas.

Just below the shoulder of the bell is another ring of vajras, this time sixteen in number. These represent the walls of the mandala palace. As we now turn our attention to the gently inclined shoulder of the bell, we have entered the palace and are in the presence of the deities it contains. On this level we find eight lotus petals interspersed with eight seed syllables. The lotus petals represent the lotus-daises on which the deities stand. Seed syllables are combinations of letters (in Sanskrit or Tibetan) that are subtle manifestations of the consciousness of a Tantric deity. Thus the seed syllable can also be used to represent the deity themselves. For instance the syllable *tam* stands for the female Bodhisattva Tara.

There are different systems of interpretation of the deities represented by the eight seed syllables. One has the eight great Bodhisattvas with their consorts (in the form of offering goddesses). Another simply has eight female Bodhisattvas. Whatever system is followed, these figures represent the wise and compassionate beings who are in attendance on the central deity.

As we continue moving inwards and upwards, we come to a ring of lotuses that emanate from the bottom of the bell's stem. On my vajra-bell there are twenty-four of them. These form the lotus throne of the central deity. Next on the stem we come to four long-life vases. These are the emblem of Amitayus, the Buddha associated with longevity. They are filled with *amrita*, the nectar whose name literally means 'the deathless'. In the case of the vajra-bell, these four vases are understood to represent the body of Prajnaparamita, the central deity, which is regarded as being of the nature of nectar. This is a symbolic way of saying that Prajnaparamita grants all spiritual accomplishments. If you intuitively realize the Perfection of Wisdom, you see beyond the psychophysical organism, subject to ageing and death, with which you usually identify, and gain a glimpse of what Tantric Buddhism sometimes refers to as the deathless state. Thus although Amitayus is associated with longevity, he is concerned primarily with what transcends mundane life altogether.

Finally we come to the face of Prajnaparamita herself, smiling benignly from the upper part of the stem of the bell. She is crowned with a diadem bearing five great jewels – again representing the wisdoms of the Five Buddhas – that merges into the lotuses at the bottom of the half vajra that forms the bell's handle. This crown suggests that she has attained the totality of wisdom, and sees all aspects of ultimate reality.

Thus the bell, like the vajra, is a symbol of extraordinary richness. It incorporates both the vault of the sky of emptiness and the whole mandala – with its protective circles, palace, and deities – to which that emptiness gives birth in the mind of the Tantric meditator. However, it acquires yet more meanings when placed alongside the vajra. Now that we have explored the vajra and bell individually, it is time to examine the further symbolic dimensions that appear when they are used together.

12

VAJRA AND BELL TOGETHER

IN IMAGINATION OR REALITY, again see and feel the vajra in your right hand, and the vajra-bell in your left. Contemplate them both for a little while, trying to feel how they relate to, and complement, each other. Having allowed your own intuition about them to come into play, we shall explore their traditional symbolic meanings in Buddhist Tantra.

Imagine holding all masculine qualities in your right hand, and all feminine qualities in your left hand. As we have seen, in Buddhist Tantra the right side of the body is associated with the masculine, the left with the feminine. Thus the vajra, with its more phallic shape, is the emblem of the right side, while the hollow bell goes to the feminine left side. This is an example of the way in which symbolism changes depending on context. The bell by itself, with its vajra handle and clapper, could be seen as a symbol of integrated masculine and feminine, but when it is placed next to the vajra it becomes more definitely a symbol for the feminine. 'Masculine' and 'feminine' here have nothing much to do with biology and gender, but rather with a gender symbolism for spiritual qualities.

Now imagine holding universal compassion in your right hand and transcendental wisdom in your left hand. We are now moving closer to the real significance of the vajra and bell, towards which mundane symbols such as thunderbolts and diamonds are merely pointers. The bell stands for transcendental wisdom, *prajna*, which sees the true nature of all phenomena. That this nature is a no-nature – an open dimension, un-graspable, and devoid of any fixed, inherent existence – is symbolized by the empty space enclosed by the bell. In Tantra this wisdom is associated with the feminine, and with the left.

The vajra stands for compassion, which is expressed as skilful means (Sanskrit, *upaya*). This is the activity of wisdom. Seeing that living beings suffer unnecessarily because of their deluded perceptions of life, and recognizing that those 'living beings' are not ultimately separate from himself or herself, the Bodhisattva endowed with transcendental wisdom is impelled to act to help the suffering world. The Bodhisattva does this by practising the perfections. Thus the vajra stands for the practice of generosity, ethics, patience, effort, and meditation; the bell represents the wisdom with which these first five perfections are imbued. You can only take up the vajra and bell on the Tantric path if you are firmly committed to the Bodhisattva ideal. Indeed, the tradition is that you practise the Vajrayana as a way of attaining Buddhahood as quickly as possible, in order to be of the utmost help to all sentient beings. Although, sadly, people sometimes pursue Tantric initiation for the magical powers they believe will result, the true spirit of Buddhist Tantra is one of altruism and selflessness.

Plate 1

Plate 2.   DHARDO RIMPOCHE PERFORMING A RITUAL WITH VAJRA AND BELL

Plate 3

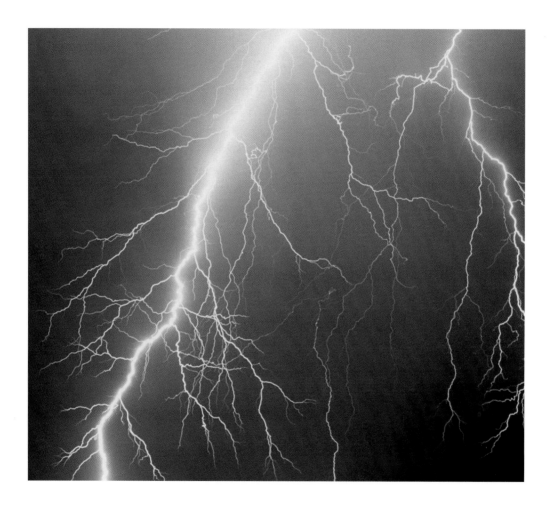

Plate 4

Plate 5

Plate 6. SOVEREIGN'S SCEPTRE WITH CROSS

Plate 7

Plate 8

13

VAJRA AND BELL IN HIGHEST TANTRA

So far we have been contemplating the general symbolism of the vajra and bell, which it is open to anyone to appreciate and use as a source of inspiration for their spiritual practice. But there is a further symbolism associated with these ritual objects, which comes from their use in the highest levels of Buddhist Tantra. As we shall see, the practices of Highest Tantra are intended for very advanced practitioners, and can be undertaken only on the basis of very considerable preparation. We may be very far from being ready to undertake these practices, but knowing a little about them will give more weight to our appreciation of the vajra and bell as symbols, and to our understanding of their meaning for the Tibetan Buddhist tradition. I shall not be going into much detail, and this section can be taken in the spirit of someone setting out on a journey who opens a map and points out to his companions the far mountain peak that they may one day reach.

So now once more experience holding the vajra and bell. Imagine that the vajra in your right hand has the quality of intense bliss, and the bell in your left hand embodies the wisdom of emptiness. This bliss is deeper and more fulfilling than anything you have ever experienced, but there is no tendency to try to hold on to it, no anxiety about it coming to an end. It is no one's possession. It is so satisfying that the mind would not dream of moving away from it. And it is with this completely stable state of mind that one understands ever more deeply the true, empty nature of things. Eventually there is just a blissful knowing, a clear-seeing bliss. Bliss and emptiness are two qualities of the same experience, inseparable.

We have now arrived at the essence of Buddhist Tantra, and the heart of the symbolism of the vajra and bell. The main reason the Vajrayana considers itself to be a quicker path than the standard Mahayana one is because it uses special methods, not found in general Mahayana teaching, for contemplating emptiness. The understanding of emptiness is the same in both Mahayana and Vajrayana; the difference is that the Tantra uses particular yogic methods to enable one to contemplate emptiness with an extremely subtle and blissful consciousness.

The main aim of Tantric methods is to contemplate emptiness – symbolized by the bell – with this mind of 'Great Bliss' – the vajra. This enables a particularly deep penetration of emptiness. Clearing the veils of emotional affliction and ignorance that obscure the sun of reality is the main work on the path to Enlightenment. Thus this practice that enables you to develop the mind of Great Bliss and then use it to contemplate emptiness is considered to be particularly efficacious for the rapid attainment of Buddhahood.

However, although we can talk of the 'rapid attainment of Buddhahood', to be in a hurry will only slow us down. Many people, on learning that Vajrayana Buddhism considers its methods to be particularly efficacious, want to cut to the Tantric chase as soon as possible. This is a serious mistake, and can even be very dangerous. One danger is that of inflation. The whole of the Dharma is designed to help one to overcome one's egotistical concerns. It is easy to latch on to the fact that one has had supposedly high initiations, or is performing practices designed for advanced meditators, and assume that one has thereby magically gained some advanced spiritual status. In actual fact one's pride in such pseudo-accomplishments means that one is even further from Enlightenment than before one took up Tantric practice.

Another danger is that, having taken up Tantric practices unprepared, and with unrealistic expectations, one may not follow them through faithfully. Discovering that they are not a magic passport to Enlightenment, and that the practices are complex, take time to learn, and require much hard work, one gives up on them. It is better not to begin with Tantric methods than to pick them up and put them down casually.

Yet another danger is that the methods of the highest levels of Tantra, wrongly applied, may lead to physical problems or mental instability. These methods affect the fundamental 'wiring' of our consciousness. While Westerners know well enough that they should not mess about carelessly with electricity, they are often very naïve when it comes to tinkering with their most subtle and powerful psychophysical energies.

One way or another, the attempt to begin with advanced practice always fails. In spiritual life you never get something for nothing. In fact it might be closer to the truth to say that in Buddhist practice you get nothing for something. All the work you put in over the years leads you to a point in which you identify with nothing in particular at all. You lose your own soul, in the sense of letting go of a sense of inherent selfhood, and thereby gain the whole world, feeling connected to everything.

So, to reiterate, in this section I am describing methods that can be used successfully only after a great deal of prior preparation. First you have to practise the general Buddhist path until you have attained a good degree of stability in your Dharma practice, and in particular have developed a strong degree of motivation to follow the Bodhisattva path. Then you need to find a qualified Tantric teacher who is prepared to give you initiation into the Anuttarayoga, or highest level of Tantra, along with the relevant meditation instructions. Only then can you follow what are known as the paths of *kyerim* and *dzogrim*.

Kyerim means 'generation stage'. In this you learn to identify yourself with a Tantric deity. The aim of Tantra is to resolve the deluded and divisive concepts that we impose on our experience. Someone may think of themselves as Beth or Mike, and feel they are separate from the world around them. If they practise the Generation Stage of Highest Tantra, they will be taught to do away with ordinary appearances by visualizing themselves as the deity within the mandala. If they do this on the basis of a good understanding of emptiness, they will gradually replace their concept of being Beth or Mike with being Tara, Hevajra, or whichever Tantric deity they focus on. In this way, by degrees, ordinary appearances and the deluded concepts that accompany them are overcome.

In practising the visualizations of the Generation Stage, you have to learn and be able to visualize all the details, such as the colour, posture, hand implements, surrounding figures, and mandala palace. As well as developing this very detailed visual image, you also need to generate the divine pride of feeling that you *are* the deity: Cakrasamvara, Vajrabhairava, Vajrayogini, or whoever it may be.

Once the 'clear appearance' of the deity and the mandala have been stabilized, along with the 'divine pride' of being the deity, you have to practise visualizing the whole mandala in a very minute size. This further refines the meditating consciousness. Finally, when this very subtle mandala visualization is stable, and can be concentrated upon without mental wavering for hours at a time, you have fulfilled the requirements for moving from the *kyerim* to the *dzogrim*.

Dzogrim means 'completion stage' or 'fulfilment stage'. In the generation stage you were, to a large extent, refining your mind by the use of imagination. Thus at certain points in the generation stage meditation you would dissolve away the visualization of the deity and mandala, and imagine yourself developing a mind of Great Bliss with which you would meditate on emptiness. However, this Great Bliss would not be the real thing, but an imagined sense of what the experience of Great Bliss would be like. In the completion stage, through working with extremely subtle psychophysical energies, you bring about the true experience of Great Bliss. With this genuine experience of Great Bliss you then contemplate emptiness. This extirpates from the subtlest levels of the mind the tendency to misconstrue the nature of reality.

This process of refining consciousness until finally you experience its subtlest level, which is also the level of most intense blissfulness, is not an easy one. It involves consciously going through the stages of withdrawal from the physical body and senses that happen naturally at the time of death. The advanced meditator may well stop breathing during deep samadhi or concentration. It is as if you deliberately let go of the samsaric world of the physical body, consciously go through the death process, arrive at the subtlest level of consciousness, employ that to meditate on emptiness and to experience reality itself, and then, rather than the uncontrolled rebirth that unenlightened people take, you take rebirth as a Buddha for the benefit of all beings.

This whole process is symbolized by the vajra and bell. For instance, the vajra can be interpreted in a completely different way from that which we looked at earlier. The yoga of the Completion Stage involves moving deeper within the body of the deity to visualize a whole subtle 'physiology' (or what would correspond to physiology on the physical plane). First, you need to meditate on a whole system of 'channels', 'winds', and 'drops'. Once this is clearly seen you manipulate it in various ways to bring about radical changes in consciousness. In particular you visualize the central channel, and two main side channels, within which the 'winds', or subtle energies, move. These side channels also constrict the central channel in various ways. The meditator's task, from the Tantric point of view, is to loosen the constrictions on the central channel, and to cause the energy winds increasingly to enter it until their tendency to move in the side channels is overcome.

The structure of the vajra can be interpreted in terms of this 'subtle physiology'. For instance, the central axis running the length of the vajra stands for the central channel. The eight surrounding prongs that emanate from it stand for the eight channels that come out from the heart centre. The rings on either side of the central hub stand for constrictions of the central channel that have to be loosened. The central hub represents the 'indestructible drop' – the most subtle consciousness that Buddhist Tantra believes passes from one life to the next – at the heart centre.

Thus the vajra stands for the whole process of bringing the winds into the central channel and bringing about the experience of Great Bliss that is generated through that process. The bell represents the emptiness on which you meditate with that subtle blissful consciousness. This is their primary significance for the Tantra. However, there is still one stage further to go in looking at these incredibly rich symbols.

14

THE VAJRAHUMKARA MUDRA

YOU ARE STILL holding the vajra in your right hand and the bell in your left. Now cross your hands over your chest, with the right hand outermost, and with the forefinger and little finger of each hand extended. This is perhaps the quintessential Tantric mudra or symbolic gesture, known as the *vajrahumkara* mudra. A major aspect of its symbolism concerns the union of opposites. The right hand goes to the left side; the left hand to the right. The vajra and bell each move, as it were, into the natural domain of the other.

This symbolism of the union of opposites appears everywhere in Tantra. The vajra and bell themselves both incorporate it. The bell itself has a vajra-handle. The vajra has at its centre an egg of emptiness. The symbolism of this mudra reinforces the message that the seeming polarities of the vajra and bell are not separate.

In the early stages of the Buddhist path, wisdom and compassion may be separate experiences, but at the Tantric level they become two aspects of one experience. Similarly, the visualized deity and the surrounding mandala are also understood to be not really separate but seamless manifestations of consciousness. At the highest Tantric stages the extremely subtle blissful consciousness and the wisdom of emptiness also become non-dual. The use of the vajra and bell symbolizes, promotes, and reinforces all these understandings.

15

RITUAL USES OF THE VAJRA AND BELL

PRACTITIONERS OF the Highest Tantra have a commitment to keep a vajra and bell with them at all times – though when this is inconvenient the commitment can be fulfilled by using a representation of them instead. The vajra and bell are sacred objects – not in the sense of being associated with a creator god, but because they symbolize and help to develop the realization of ultimate reality. They should always be treated with awareness and respect, as this helps to reinforce their effectiveness as ritual objects. Vajra-bells should not be used outside the ritual context, and when handling them one should avoid putting one's fingers across the face of Prajnaparamita.

In Tantric ritual the vajra and bell are omnipresent, usually placed on a small table in front of the lama or other practitioner, along with the other ritual implements. In some rituals, such as fire pujas, the practitioner must take up the vajra and bell at the beginning of the ritual and not put them down until the end.

When looking at the vajra-bell earlier, we saw some of the ritual uses to which the vajra and bell may be put. In general they serve as symbolic physical embodiments of the state of mind the ritual aims to promote. The vajra as royal sceptre is a reminder that the Tantric meditator has to let go of ordinary appearances and concepts and maintain the appearance and conception of himself or herself as the Tantric deity. The vajra-bell is a constant reminder that that Tantric deity has no inherent existence, but is a manifestation of emptiness.

The vajra and bell also have the effect of reminding the practitioner that everything that happens within the magic circle of the ritual is sacred. It is as if, holding the vajra and bell, everything the Tantric ritualist touches turns to diamond – the diamond of the true nature of reality. For instance, with vajra and bell in hand, the meditator may make various offerings to a visualized assembly of Buddhist figures. These offerings may include such things as flowers, incense, and lights. These offerings are usually represented by hand gestures. The presence of the vajra and bell in the hands as the mudras are made (and the mudras are all designed to allow them to be performed while holding ritual implements) serves as a reminder that you are not offering ordinary gifts. Instead you are offering vajra-flowers, vajra-incense, and so on. The offerings are seen as surpassingly beautiful, like diamonds, and are offered with an awareness of their ultimately empty nature.

16

THE DOUBLE VAJRA

NOW THAT WE have completed our exploration of the symbolism of the vajra and bell, for the sake of completeness we need to look at some other contexts in which the vajra appears in Buddhist Tantra. Perhaps the most important of these manifestations we need to consider is the double vajra. This consists of two crossed vajras, sharing a common hub. In Sanskrit this powerful symbol is known as the *vishvavajra* – *vishva* meaning 'all' or 'everything'. Double vajras are not used as ritual hand implements, but they appear in several other contexts in Tantric Buddhism.

First, they appear in many situations where there is an emphasis on stability. Placed horizontally, their four half-vajras in the four directions give the crossed vajra tremendous strength and firmness. Thus it is associated with the earth, and a firm foundation. Crossed vajras are visualized as the unshakeable foundations of the mandala palace. Bodh Gaya, where the historical Buddha gained Enlightenment, is known as the vajra seat (Sanskrit, *vajrasana*). When he sat to meditate there under the bodhi tree, the Buddha made an absolute commitment to gain Enlightenment or die, saying, 'Flesh may wither, blood may dry up, but I shall not leave this spot until I am enlightened.' The double vajra is a fine symbol for the stability of mind that comes from total commitment.

Secondly, the four half-vajras of the crossed vajra are related to the four Tantric activities. In Buddhist Tantra, once you have become identified with the energy of a particular Buddha or Bodhisattva through visualization and mantra recitation, you can employ the spiritual energy you have gained for positive purposes – either for your own welfare, or in order to benefit others. First, the energy may be used to pacify hindrances and obstacles. Secondly, it may be employed to increase positive qualities such as one's lifespan, one's virtuous activities, or one's wisdom. Thirdly, it can be used in what is known as fascinating or magnetizing. This involves drawing towards yourself situations helpful to your progress on the Path, as well as making you more capable of drawing others to the Dharma. Fourthly, the energy may be used to destroy obstacles and negative tendencies.

When the crossed vajra is depicted pictorially, the central hub is usually depicted in blue, representing the Buddha Akshobhya. The parts in the four directions are painted in white, yellow, red, and green, to represent the other four Buddhas of the mandala. White is thus associated with pacification, yellow (the colour of gold and the harvest) with increase, red (the colour of warmth and the most striking and noticeable of all colours) with attraction or fascination, and green with destruction.

These four Tantric rites relate quite closely to the four right efforts found in Pali

Buddhism. These involve encouraging positive mental states that have not previously arisen to arise, developing further those positive states that have already arisen, preventing from arising negative states that have not arisen, and eliminating negative mental states that have arisen. There are two differences of emphasis, however. The Tantric activities operate on an almost magical level, employing the power of the Tantric deity, whereas the four right efforts are developed on the basis of the everyday self. Secondly, the Vajrayana being based in the Bodhisattva ideal, the Tantric activities are performed primarily for the welfare of other sentient beings.

The five-coloured double vajra is often represented on brocade hangings adorning the teaching thrones of high lamas. By implication, it suggests they are seated in the place of the Buddha. Within the Tantric context this is true, as the lama is often regarded as a Buddha, and it is only through him that one can hear the Buddha's teaching. In the West, unfortunately, the whole teaching of 'guru as Buddha' is problematic, as Westerners will often have unrealistic expectations of their teachers, and enter into a fantasy relationship with them. Although it is based very much on magical principles, correct Tantric practice is always very grounded and realistic.

Finally, the crossed vajra is the emblem of the Buddha Amoghasiddhi, whose name means 'Unobstructed Success'. He is the green Buddha who is associated with the north of the mandala and the air element. In particular, he is the embodiment of the all-accomplishing wisdom. He is represented as making the gesture of fearlessness with his right hand. Often his left hand rests in his lap, in the gesture of meditation, with the crossed vajra in its palm. Amoghasiddhi is the most mysterious of the Five Buddhas. He is associated with midnight, and the bringing together of opposites. Clearly the vishvavajra is a fine symbol for the union of all opposites whatsoever.

Amoghasiddhi could be characterized as the most active of the Five Buddhas. His all-accomplishing wisdom represents the enlightened mind's impact on the world. We could say that the task of a Buddha is to build a Pure Land, an environment in which sentient beings have the best possible conditions in which to practise the Dharma and achieve Enlightenment in their turn. Perhaps something of this task, and its successful accomplishment, is suggested by Amoghasiddhi's emblem of the crossed vajra, for the crossed vajra represents both the unshakeable foundation of wisdom on which that Pure Land needs to be built, and the four Tantric activities by which the Buddha will destroy the obstacles of sentient beings, pacify their hindrances, attract them to the Dharma, and increase their wisdom and compassion until Enlightenment is finally obtained.

17

RITUAL IMPLEMENTS AND MANDALAS

AS THE VAJRA is the central symbol of Tantric Buddhism, it naturally appears in many different contexts. We shall look at some of these in this section.

Buddhist Tantra makes much use of the visualization of wrathful deities. These embody heroic qualities, states of mind in which one musters great energy in the service of the Dharma. These wrathful figures are usually depicted brandishing weapons (all of which are understood to represent positive spiritual qualities that overcome or destroy negative mental states). Perhaps the most common of these implements is the vajra-chopper (Sanskrit, *kartika*). This is a knife with a curved blade used by butchers. It works both as a chopper and as a flaying knife. It is held in the right hand by many dakinis (ecstatic female figures) and some wrathful deities, such as Vajrabhairava and some forms of Mahakala. The chopper has a vajra-handle, and being held in the right hand, as we shall see later, it symbolizes the skilful means through which wisdom is given compassionate expression. Thus the vajra-chopper is a symbol for the compassionate severing of all ignorance and negativity. It is quite a weighty implement, and its cutting off of ignorance has all the finality of the sound of a butcher's chopper hitting the chopping board. As a flaying knife it strips the skin from mundane existence, revealing the guts of suffering beneath its superficially attractive appearance.

Many other implements are adorned with vajras. In Tantric visualizations you may come upon a vajra-hammer, a sword with a vajra-handle (wielded, for example, by Manjushri, the Bodhisattva of wisdom), a vajra-axe, and so on. As well as carrying vajra-implements, Tantric deities are often dressed in vajra-ornaments. Some are adorned with necklaces of vajras. Others wear them as ornaments on their crown. For instance, the dakini Vajrayogini has a crown ornament made of bone that is surmounted by a half vajra. Her consort Cakrasamvara has a crossed vajra adorning his hair. Many wrathful deities wear ornaments of human bone in the shape of vajras. These all have symbolic meanings, but inasmuch as the vajra is always a symbol for the true nature of things, these ornaments in general stand for the fact that all the experience of the deity is imbued with the clarity that understands all phenomena as they really are.

As well as their use as implements, vajras are often the building blocks in 'Tantric architecture'. We have seen already how the mandala is protected by a fence and canopy made of vajras. In addition, the floor of the deity's palace is constructed of vajras, whilst miraculously remaining flat and smooth to the touch. The walls and upper reaches of the palace are also constructed of vajras, and the entire mandala will have a vajra fence protecting it. Although these vajras provide an invulnerable protection, we must not think of them as solid and heavy. Like everything else in the mandala, they are made of light. It is understood in Tantric practice that everything is a mental creation, and this helps accustom the mind to seeing the everyday world in the same way, like a dream, empty and ungraspable.

Sometimes large vajras are constructed. At Samye Monastery in Tibet, built in the time of Padmasambhava, there is a giant vajra that is said to have flown by itself over the Himalayas from India. This vajra reputedly formed the pattern for all representations of the vajra in Tibet. This story may be a mythologization of the fact that the symbol of the vajra was originally brought to Tibet from India.

18

HOLDERS OF THE VAJRA

NO CONSIDERATION of the vajra and bell can be complete without at least a short look at the various figures in Mahayana and Tantra who are represented holding a vajra and / or vajra-bell. As I have covered this ground at length in *Meeting the Buddhas*, I shall give only a brief survey here, before focusing on one representative figure.

In principle, any of six main classes of figures visualized in Tantric Buddhism may have vajras among their emblems. For instance, Tantric gurus are often given the epithet 'vajra-guru' and many are represented holding a vajra. Padmasambhava is credited with helping to establish Buddhism in Tibet, and is the central teacher for the Nyingma School of Tibetan Buddhism. He is commonly depicted with a vajra in his right hand, his forefinger and little finger extended in order to ward off demons and obstacles.

Among the *yidams* of Highest Yoga Tantra (complex figures who embody the whole path of practice of a particular Tantric text or set of texts) many hold the vajra and bell crossed as they embrace their consorts. One example is the yidam Cakrasamvara, sometimes known as Heruka. He is a deep blue figure, often with twelve arms, representing the understanding of the twelve *nidanas* or 'links' of the process by which things arise in dependence upon conditions. He embraces his female consort, the brilliant red Vajrayogini, in sexual union, his hands crossed behind her back, holding the vajra and bell.

Among the Buddhas, Akshobhya is particularly associated with the vajra. He is head of the Vajra family in the mandala. He is the deep blue of the sky at altitude, and is depicted seated cross-legged with his left hand in his lap, often with an upright golden vajra in its palm, and his right hand against his right knee, fingers downward, in the mudra of touching the earth. His name means 'the Immovable', which relates to the vajra's diamond qualities.

Among the great Bodhisattvas, Vajrapani is always depicted with the vajra. He appears in a peaceful, pale blue form, in which case he holds the vajra-sceptre to his heart, or alternatively holds the stem of a lotus that opens at shoulder level with an upright vajra on its calyx. In his wrathful form he is massive, deep blue, surrounded by an aura of wisdom flames, and is brandishing, or preparing to hurl, a vajra in his upraised right hand.

Of the dakas and dakinis, the wild heroes and heroines of the Tantra who are sources of inspiration and sometimes messengers from higher spiritual levels, many are represented with either vajra or bell. Take for example Machig Labdrön. She was a Tibetan woman who was one of the founders of the tradition of Tantric practice known as *Chöd*, which means 'cutting off'. In this practice you work to overcome attachment to the body (and therefore fear of death) by visualizing that your body becomes transformed into an offering to all beings. Machig Labdrön is frequently represented in Tibetan art in the form of a white dancing dakini, wild and ecstatic, playing a large damaru (often known as a Chöd drum) in her right hand and a vajra-bell in her left.

Among the dharmapalas too, the protectors of the Dharma, the vajra makes frequent appearances as a weapon for warding off enemies of the Dharma.

19

THE BUDDHA VAJRADHARA

HAVING SURVEYED the various orders of Tantric figures, let us now look more closely at one figure. We shall meet the Buddha Vajradhara, whose name means 'Holder of the Vajra'. The Tibetans believe that the tantras were taught by the Buddha Shakyamuni, appearing in the form of Vajradhara. For some schools of Tibetan Buddhism Vajradhara is the so-called 'adi-Buddha' or primordial Buddha. However, we need to be careful not to take the idea of a 'primordial Buddha' literally. It is not that there is a Buddha called Vajradhara who appeared at the beginning of time (perhaps even as some kind of creator of the universe). The adi-Buddha is 'primordial' in the sense that he represents the fact that Enlightenment is always a potential for consciousness. That potential has existed since beginningless time. It is inherent in the nature of the universe. The path to Enlightenment may become lost and forgotten, but eventually it will be rediscovered by another Buddha, who will teach the Dharma. The Tibetan belief is that only certain Buddhas will teach Tantra, so they regard the opportunity to take up the vajra and bell and utilize the Tantric methods of self-transformation as particularly valuable.

As with any visualization, we need first to meditate on the empty nature of reality. Sometimes mantras are used to evoke awareness of this reality. One of the most common for this purpose is *om shunyata jnana vajra svabhava atmako 'ham*. This can be translated as 'Om. I am the very self whose essence is the diamond of the knowledge of Emptiness.'[16]

A mantra such as this evokes the experience of empty space, which is the best symbol we have for shunyata, inasmuch as space is uncompounded. It cannot be divided.

Out of the blue sky appears a lotus throne, made of lotus petals of various colours. On the lotus appears a moon mat. The blue sky above the moon mat starts to become darker, with scintillating points of colour. Gradually from the sky appears a deep blue Buddha, his body adorned with various jewels. He is seated cross-legged in meditation, in the position known in Tantric Buddhism as the vajra posture. His crossed legs, with each foot resting on the opposite thigh, suggest the double vajra. It is also the most stable of all sitting postures, and because bodily posture and mental state are related, it suggests the absolute stability of the mind of the Buddha.

The Buddha's body is adorned with silks and jewelled ornaments. These are the adornments of the Bodhisattva, and suggest that the Buddha has completed the entire

Bodhisattva path, and in particular that he has developed to the highest degree the great Bodhisattva qualities: generosity, ethics, patience, effort, meditation, and wisdom. These positive mental states are intensely beautiful, and affect everyone with whom he comes into contact, just as people are attracted by jewels and beautiful clothing. On his head the Buddha wears a five-jewelled crown, symbolizing his perfectly developed wisdoms of the Five Buddhas – the mirror-like wisdom and so forth.

Great auras of light around his body and head emphasize that he has completed the two accumulations. These are the accumulation of merit and wisdom. We could say that through the accumulation of merit the Buddha's consciousness has become a continuous flow of positive mental states, overflowing with generosity, patience, and so on. Through the accumulation of wisdom he has come to see that those mental states, and all phenomena, are not the possession of any kind of fixed self. These two accumulations enable the Buddha to enter into extraordinary samadhis or states of transcendental concentration, and to perform all kinds of feats which for us, trapped in the straitjacket of a fixed self-view, and blindfolded by a belief that we are confronted by an objective world of truly-existent phenomena, seem miraculous.

The Buddha's hands are crossed in the vajrahumkara mudra. Between the thumb and palm of each hand appears the top of a vajra, so that it appears he is holding two vajras. But really he is holding a vajra and a bell, the bottom of the bell being hidden behind his right wrist. The vajra and bell symbolize the Buddha's perfect mastery of the Tantric path. He has perfected the generation and completion stages, visualizing himself unwaveringly and with flawless concentration as the deity within the mandala. He has also practised visualizing the channels, winds, and drops, loosened all the knots in the central channel, and caused all the energy winds to enter into and abide in the central channel. Through this he has developed the mind of Great Bliss. With this subtle and intensely blissful consciousness he has meditated on emptiness and put paid to all doubts and delusions about the nature of reality. Out of this deep samadhi he has allowed his consciousness to appear in the form of a Buddha in order to teach the path to Enlightenment for the sake of all beings. All these meanings are conveyed by the vajra and bell in the crossed blue hands.

CONCLUSION

AS WE SAW earlier, one of the fundamental principles of Tantric meditation is that it aims at total self-transformation. Tantric practices usually involve body, speech, and mind, in order to ensure that the positive qualities you develop in meditation do not stay on a purely mental level, but are carried into all aspects of your humanity, right down to your fingertips. Therefore it puts into the hands of its dedicated practitioners symbols of their highest values. Holding the vajra and bell, it is as if you can see and touch skilful means and wisdom, Great Bliss and emptiness, and employ them for the benefit of all sentient beings.

If you are not engaged in Tantric practice, you can still gain great inspiration from these beautiful symbols. Contemplating them you can come to understand a great deal about the Buddhist path to Enlightenment. In the course of this book we have seen that the vajra and bell are not two cold metallic objects, but symbols that reach to the very heart of our potential as human beings. May contemplating them help each one of us to follow the path of the Dharma, and to become sources of wisdom and compassion for the world.

NOTES AND REFERENCES

1   Published by Serindia, London n.d.
2   *Meeting The Buddhas: A Guide to Buddhas, Bodhisattvas and Tantric Deities*, Windhorse, Birmingham, 1998.
3   In Western Europe the thunder cult became very prominent during the Neolithic period, though it may have begun much earlier.
4   Trungpa says that Indra's thunderbolt, which had a hundred prongs, was made from the bones of a sage who had meditated on Mount Meru for centuries. When the sage died, his bones were turned into a vajra. See *The Tibetan Book of the Dead: The Great Liberation Through Hearing in the Bardo*, translated with commentary by Francesca Fremantle and Chögyam Trungpa, Shambhala, Boulder and London, 2000, p.17.
5   *Ambattha Sutta*, Digha Nikaya 3. See Maurice Walshe (trans.), *Long Discourses of the Buddha*, Wisdom Publications, Boston 1995, p.116.
6   For a clear and very useful summary of the development of Indian Buddhist Tantra see Chapter 7 (by Anthony Tribe) of Paul Williams with Anthony Tribe, *Buddhist Thought: A Complete Introduction to the Indian Tradition*, Routledge, London and New York, 2000.
7   For a detailed account of the mandala of the Five Buddhas see Part 2 of *Meeting the Buddhas*, op. cit.
8   For an account of this development, see David Snellgrove, *Indo-Tibetan Buddhism*, Serindia, London 1987, pp.134 *et seq.*
9   Peter Masefield (trans.), *Udana* 8.iii, Pali Text Society, Oxford 1997, p.166.
10 Trungpa, op. cit., p.17.

11 Robert Moore and Douglas Gillette, *King, Warrior, Magician, Lover: Rediscovering the Archetypes of the Mature Masculine*, Harper SanFrancisco, 1991.
12 For more on the eight great Bodhisattvas, see chapter 17 of *Meeting The Buddhas*, which is devoted to them.
13 In different tantras the Buddhas and their consorts are arranged in various ways within the mandala. I am following the system outlined in the *Bardo Thödol*, commonly known as the *Tibetan Book of the Dead.*
14 See Chapter 20 of *Meeting The Buddhas* for details of Vajrasattva and the Vajrasattva mantra.
15 See chapter 19 of *Meeting The Buddhas.*
16 Translated by Stephan Beyer in *The Cult of Tara: Magic and Ritual in Tibet*, University of California Press, California and London, 1978.

INDEX

A

adi-Buddha 53
adornments 54
Akashadhateshvari 22
Akshobhya 6, 21, 46, 52
Ambattha 5
Ambattha Sutta 4, 57
Amitabha 21
Amitayus 33
Amoghasiddhi 21, 47
amrita 33
animitta samadhi 19
Anthony Abbot, St 26
Anuttarayoga *see* Highest Tantra
apranihita samadhi 19
archetypes 17
Avalokiteshvara 32

B

bell 23, 25ff
bliss 38, 40f

Bodh Gaya 45
Bodhicitta 20
Bodhisattva 20, 36
Bodhisattvas, eight great 33, 58
body, in Tantra 17, 28, 35
Buddha 4, 5, 53
    primordial 53
Buddhism 9

C

Cakrasamvara 50, 51
Carya Tantra 5
channels 41
Chöd 52
circles of protection 31ff
compassion 36
completion stage 40f
compounded 10
conditioned 10
coronation 16, 17

crocodile 21
Cronus 4

D
damaru 2, 52
danger 38
deathless state 33
dharmata 19
diamond 9f
Diamond Sutra 5
directionlessness 19
doors of liberation 19
dorje 12, *see also* vajra
double vajra 45ff
drum 2, 52
dzogrim 40

E
efforts, four right 46
eight great Bodhisattvas 33, 58
emptiness 20, 28f, 31, 54
energy 46
equanimity 19

F
Family Protectors 32
Four Great Initiations 16
four right efforts 46
four Tantric rites 45

G
generation stage 39
Gillette, D. 17
Great Bliss 38, 40f
guru 47

H
Heruka 51
Highest Tantra 6, 37

I
impermanence 10, 13, 19
Indra 4, 57
Initiations, Four Great 16
insight 14, 15, *see also prajna*, wisdom

K
Kalu Rimpoche 1
kartika 49
king, archetype 17
Kriya Tantra 5
kyerim 39

L
lama 47
lightning 14
Locana 21
lotus 32
lover, archetype 17

M
Machig Labdrön 52
magician, archetype 17
Mahakala 49
mahasiddha 13
makara 21, 32
Mamaki 21
mandala 5, 30, 50
   in vajra-bell 30ff
Manjushri 32, 50
mantra 5

Mantrayana 5
Meeting the Buddhas 3
mindfulness bell 26
Moore, R. 17
mudra 42, 44

O
offerings 44
orb 16

P
Padmasambhava 50, 51
Pandaravasini 21
perfections, six 20, 36
philosopher's stone 12f
prajna 14, 15, 36, *see also* wisdom
Prajnaparamita 28, 33
Pure Land 47

R
Ratnasambhava 21
reality 19

S
Samye Ling 1
Samye Monastery 50
sceptre 16
seed syllable 33
self 20
selfhood, lack of 20
Shakyamuni 4, 53
shunyata *see* emptiness
shunyata samadhi 20
siddhi 13
signlessness 19

skilful means 36
sky 29
sound 23
space 54
suffering 19, 22f, 38
symbolism 37

T
Tantra 5, 36, 39
   Carya 5
   Highest 6, 37
   Kriya 5
Tantric guru 51
Tantric initiation 17
Tantric rites 45
Tara 21, 33
Thor 4, 15
three circles of protection 31ff
three doors of liberation 19
Three Family Protectors 32
three marks 15, 19
thunder cult 57
thunderbolt 4, 14f, 57
transformation 12f, 56
two accumulations 55

U
union of opposites 42
unsatisfactoriness 19, *see also* suffering
upaya 36

V
Vairocana 21
Vajirapani 4, 5
Vajra Master initiation 16

vajra, attributes 15
  -chopper 49
  double 45ff
  -guru 51
Vajrabhairava 49
Vajracchedika 5
Vajradhara 6, 53ff
Vajradhatu Mandala 6, 21
vajrahumkara mudra 42
Vajrapani 6, 32, 52
vajrasana 45
Vajrasattva 26
Vajrayana 6, 38
Vajrayogini 50, 51

vase initiation 16
vishvavajra 45
visualization 29, 40ff, 53

W
warrior, archetype 17
wisdom 33, 35, *see also prajna*
Wisdoms, Five 21
wrathful deities 49

Y
yaksha 6

Z
Zeus 4, 15

The Windhorse symbolizes the energy of the enlightened mind carrying the Three Jewels –
the Buddha, the Dharma, and the Sangha – to all sentient beings.

Buddhism is one of the fastest-growing spiritual traditions in the Western world.
Throughout its 2,500-year history, it has always succeeded in adapting its mode of expression
to suit whatever culture it has encountered.

Windhorse Publications aims to continue this tradition as Buddhism comes to the West.
Today's Westerners are heirs to the entire Buddhist tradition, free to draw instruction and
inspiration from all the many schools and branches. Windhorse publishes works by authors
who not only understand the Buddhist tradition but are also familiar with Western culture
and the Western mind. Manuscripts welcome.

For orders and catalogues please write to

WINDHORSE PUBLICATIONS
11 PARK ROAD
BIRMINGHAM
B13 8AB
UK

WINDHORSE BOOKS
P O BOX 574
NEWTOWN
NSW 2042
AUSTRALIA

WEATHERHILL INC
41 MONROE TURNPIKE
TRUMBULL
CT 06611
USA

Windhorse Publications is an arm of the Friends of the Western Buddhist Order, which has more than sixty centres on five continents. Through these centres, members of the Western Buddhist Order offer regular programmes of events for the general public and for more experienced students. These include meditation classes, public talks, study on Buddhist themes and texts, and 'bodywork' classes such as t'ai chi, yoga, and massage. The FWBO also runs several retreat centres and the Karuna Trust, a fund-raising charity that supports social welfare projects in the slums and villages of India.

Many FWBO centres have residential spiritual communities and ethical businesses associated with them. Arts activities are encouraged too, as is the development of strong bonds of friendship between people who share the same ideals. In this way the FWBO is developing a unique approach to Buddhism, not simply as a set of techniques, less still as an exotic cultural interest, but as a creatively directed way of life for people living in the modern world.

If you would like more information about the FWBO please visit www.fwbo.org or write to

LONDON BUDDHIST CENTRE
51 ROMAN ROAD
LONDON
E2 OHU
UK

ARYALOKA
HEARTWOOD CIRCLE
NEWMARKET
NH 03857
USA

ALSO FROM WINDHORSE

VESSANTARA

THE MANDALA OF THE FIVE BUDDHAS

The mandala of the Five Buddhas is an important Buddhist symbol – a multi-faceted jewel communicating the different aspects of Enlightenment. Meeting each Buddha in turn, we start to awaken to the qualities they embody – energy, beauty, love, confidence, and freedom.

By contemplating the mandala as a whole we can transform ourselves through the power of the imagination, and experience the majesty of the mind set free.

Part of the series on *Buddhist symbols*

96 pages, with colour plates
ISBN 1 899579 16 8
£5.99/$11.95

VESSANTARA

MEETING THE BUDDHAS

A GUIDE TO BUDDHAS, BODHISATTVAS, AND TANTRIC DEITIES

Sitting poised and serene upon fragrant lotus blooms, they offer smiles of infinite tenderness, immeasurable wisdom. Bellowing formidable roars of angry triumph from the heart of blazing infernos, they dance on the naked corpses of their enemies.

Who are these beings – the Buddhas, Bodhisattvas, and Protectors, the 'angry demons' and 'benign deities' – of the Buddhist Tantric tradition? Are they products of an alien, even disturbed, imagination? Or are they, perhaps, real? What have they got to do with Buddhism? And what have they got to do with us?

In this vivid informed account, an experienced Western Buddhist guides us into the heart of this magical realm and introduces us to the miraculous beings who dwell there.

368 pages, with text illustrations and colour plates
ISBN 0 904766 53 5
£14.99/$29.95

KULANANDA

THE WHEEL OF LIFE

The Wheel of Life is an ancient symbol of tremendous spiritual significance. It is a graphic representation of the Buddhist understanding of life, a mirror held up to the human heart. Within its depths we see the forces that limit and bind us. We see the happiness and the suffering we create for ourselves. We see the chain of ingrained habits that makes us who we are. But, looking deeper still, we begin to see the way to freedom.

Part of the series on *Buddhist symbols*

84 pages, with illustrations
ISBN 1 899579 30 3
£5.99/$11.95

SANGHARAKSHITA

TIBETAN BUDDHISM: AN INTRODUCTION

A glorious past, a traumatic present, an uncertain future. What are we to make of Tibetan Buddhism?

Sangharakshita has spent many years in contact with Tibetan lamas of all schools, within the context of a wide experience of the Buddhist tradition as a whole. He is admirably qualified as a guide through the labyrinth that is Tibetan Buddhism. In this book he gives a down-to-earth account of the origin and history of Buddhism in Tibet, and explains the essentials of this practical tradition which has much to teach us.

As the essence of Tibetan Buddhism is revealed, it is shown to be a beautiful and noble tradition which – and this is the important thing – can help us contact a sense of beauty and nobility in our lives.

144 pages, illustrated
ISBN 0 904766 86 1
£8.50/$16.95